my name on his tongue

Arab American Writing

my name on his tongue

poems

Laila Halaby

Syracuse University Press

For a listing of books published and distributed by Syracuse University Press,
visit our Web site at SyracuseUniversityPress.syr.edu.

978-0-8156-3294-8

Library of Congress Cataloging-in-Publication Data
Halaby, Laila.
    My name on his tongue : poems / by Laila Halaby. — 1st ed.
        p. cm. — (Arab American writing)
    ISBN 978-0-8156-3294-8 (pbk. : alk. paper)
    I. Title.
    PS3608.A5455M9 2012
    811'.6—dc23   2012006950

Manufactured in the United States of America

to my mother, for giving me my story

LAILA HALABY is the author of two novels, *West of the Jordan* (2003; winner of a PEN Beyond Margins Award) and *Once in a Promised Land* (2007). She holds an undergraduate degree in Italian and Arabic from Washington University in St. Louis, a master's degree in Arabic literature from UCLA, and a master's degree in counseling from Loyola Marymount University. Halaby was the recipient of a Fulbright Scholarship for study of folklore in Jordan, which resulted in a collection of Palestinian folktales written for children. She lives with her family in Tucson, Arizona.

Contents

my grandma and your grandma were sittin' by the fire . . .

Acknowledgments

I thank the editors of the following magazines, anthologies, and websites for publishing earlier versions of these poems: *beacon broadside.com:* "open letter to president-elect Barack Obama"; *Emergences:* "freedom fighter"; *Food For Our Grandmothers:* "browner shades of white," "two women drinking coffee"; *Harmony:* "a day at the park a few days before," "penmanship"; *Mizna:* "grandfathers," "motherhood," "one day in upstate New York"; *Mr. Cogito:* "August 16, 1990"; *Poets for Palestine:* "a moonlit visit"; *rawi.org:* "letter to an Israeli soldier"; *The Poetry of Arab Women:* "handfuls of wind," "refugee"; and *Sedek* (Hebrew translation): "warning to all Arabs," "browner shades of white," and "handfuls of wind."

Thanks to Nathalie Handal and Helene Atwan, also to *Mizna*, for their support of my work. I am grateful to Khaled Mattawa for steering this collection into the generous hands of Mary Selden Evans who, along with the lovely staff at Syracuse University Press, gave this collection life. Love and thank yous to Kaiser Kuo, Rula Khalidi, and Waltraud Nichols for their valuable suggestions that helped shape this manuscript during various stages of preparation; to Houri Berberian for years of encouragement and support; to Marwan Mahmoud for always believing that my words need to be heard; to my mother, Margaret Halaby, for her support through the years and her constant and focused belief that my writing matters; and to Raad and Rabiah for the joy they bring into my life.

you can be a tourist at home

how a tour guide in Petra reminded me of all I've lost (or never had to begin with)

my name rests in the mouth of a man on horseback
reclines on his wide pink tongue
sails into the air when he rides along the wash
his red kafiyyah and white jelabiyya flapping behind
Ray Bans wrapped around his eyes
protecting them from glare and dust
my name does flips in the crisp air
bounces a few times before settling down
nestling between cheek and gum
seeping through the wet skin of his mouth
surging madly throughout his body

squeezed inside a month in my husband's
promised-by-God-to-someone-else's country
were five days in my father's never-promised-to-me land
my children and I headed south in an air conditioned car
nodded to the soft beats of a Kuwaiti singer
as we passed untidy heaps of my injured memories

from north to south it will never be mine
except in the form of a tourist attraction
I've made a life for myself elsewhere
a settled urban family
away from the familiar dark faces
dark eyes
away from the desert
the extra heartbeats
the fingers that hold on
the mouths that say
I belong here

my name lives in the mouth
of a man on horseback

you have been gone
but you are still one of us
the branch stays close to its roots
you are a good mother
a good woman, if I may be so bold
I am sure your husband is a good man
but I too would have treated you well
if I had been given the opportunity

I know you've already forgotten
with the thousands of puffy pink foreigners
you lead in and out of this ancient city
—teeming with trinkets and Bedouin—
with whom you exchange the same promises
of exclusivity

I will not forget
for in those few minutes
when you scrambled
to make yourself a memory
(and a few extra dinars)
all that is not mine
overwhelmed me
took my breath away

I can take you everywhere
you will see this place
like no one else has
when I'm done
I will take you on horseback

4

to the door
of your hotel
I've never done it before
but for you
I will do it
for you
bint al-Arab
I will take the risk
please let me

too late
there is no rewind
no re-crossing borders
oceans
going back
having it the way I wished for
too many years ago
so it will have to be like this:
my name on your tongue
between your lips

keep it there
shout it again and again
as you ride along the wash
let your voice rise above the trees
so that my name will reach the blue above
sneak into a cloud
rain down
so flecks and bits of me can stay
to nourish my land

let a drop of my name
stay in your mouth

always
taste all that you eat
but please
if you kiss a foreign woman
hide it under your tongue
or swallow it
so that I am not accidentally taken away again

you have already forgotten
are leading other fools down the bright path
spinning tales for their enjoyment

I am with you
have slipped inside your jelabiyya
cling to your bare chest
listen to your heart beat
let it become my own
I will stay here
even as my life resumes
its predictable decent pace
thousands of miles away

no matter how much zaatar you eat
you still gotta work to be an
Arab/writer/woman

the journey

born

out of place
a single mother's only child
fatherless
blanketed in foreignness

my mother ran
from one desert to another
until she found home

alone
we were opposites in a small house
me, loud and moving
wild with a longing
I didn't speak fluently
she, quiet and still
stashing her multilingual sorrows
in the tool shed out back

she tried to teach me in American
how to be an Arab
but didn't get it quite right
left stuff out
left me uncomfortable
in my shoes
always searching
for the right pair

I found them in high school
all by myself
no flour-white fairy godmother to guide me
no handsome dark prince to slide them
on my delicate size five feet

these shoes were
all me
all mine
white leather
size eight
with a star and crescent carved out
etched in silver
they curved up at the toes
genie shoes
I could disappear if I wanted to
and I did

away from the main-line mold
of A-line skirts
preppy shirts
making out after football games
I spat all of America out
like a giant wad of chewing tobacco
begged my shoes to carry me home

I spoke with an accent
played my born-in-Lebanon trump card
sailed on the fact that my father
and six half-brothers and sisters
were still There

my life became rich
with the world's tragedies
(Palestine and South Africa)
while my American connections frayed
and I finished them off
with my massive superior dagger
one by one
until they were gone

first Sara
the Jewish girl
once my best friend
who told me that Arabs were barbarians
called me fat-Arab-slime-girl

chop

then Shawna
(we used to bake
chocolate chip cookies together)

chop

even Nina
(she taught me dancing)

chop

I kept Kaiser
(he was Chinese
after all)

and Annie
(she was half Mexican
we had grown up together
were like sisters on good days)

I added Jommana
and Rula
Murad
then Hania
Mona
Marwan
and Saeed
Anoushka
Azzam
and Marcelino
Elias
Fethi
Resat
and Nora
Katia
Hassan
and Ala

I taught my tongue to dance
in Spanish
Italian
French
and Arabic
with snatches of Turkish
Greek
and Persian
unaccented and sloppy in each

I cremated my Americanness
flung it from the top of the castle in Ajlun
tossed it into the Dead Sea
drowned it off a boat in Aqaba
buried it near the ruins in Um Qais

2
___

I wrote
in a windy city in the north of Jordan

collected stories
memories
histories
got adopted by a 'real' family
visited villages
schools
refugee camps

my adjectives
changed daily
(depending
on who was watching)
American
Arab
Palestinian
Jordanian
retarded
Spanish
Christian
Muslim
deaf

Italian
Algerian

I vomited labels
(not one agreed with me)
devoured rich and fatty stories
(this kept my weight balanced)

suitcases heavy with zaatar and coffee
I returned to the States
wrote
went to school
kept writing
dipped my bread in olive oil
wrote more
kept studying
boiled my coffee three times
got married
had babies
continued writing
demanded validation
as a woman
as an Arab
as a writer

and then

when no one wanted my stories
and no one cared where I was born
where my father was from
why I looked the way I did
I walked away from my constant scribbling
sat myself at the back of the smelly city bus that is life

and accepted that I had become
exactly who I always wanted to be:
a normal person whose labels
were irrelevant

3
---

until

one sweet, quiet morning
curled up asleep with my younger child
the world imploded

people shrouded in religion
and stuffed in planes
took away our collective human breath

some people got theirs back faster than others

our grief
got cut short
by stares
over-zealous security guards
by silence
followed by hatred
the same kind that fuels people
to get on planes and fly into buildings

I unfolded my familial pledge of normalcy
and not-devoting-hours-to-imaginary-people
studied it
smoothed out the wrinkles
pressed it between the covers of a book
not the Bible

or the Quran
I stashed my promise between the pages
of *Cry the Beloved Country*
the book that taught me the power of words

in spite of my over-stuffed reality
already at bursting with
two young children
a house
a husband
a day job
I searched for a publisher
sent off poems and manuscripts
and I wrote
even though it meant
waking up just after four
when sometimes I hadn't slept until midnight
and my younger child had woken up
twice in the night

4
—

this time

everything worked out nicely
my book looked great in print
my contract for a second book was generous
requests came in
from all over the world
to hear what I had to say

but really
nothing changed

being
published
did not make me a writer
eating zaatar
did not make me an Arab
getting married and having children
did not make me a woman

I have been
all of those things
the whole time I've been sitting here
at the back of the stinky city bus
(by choice, in spite of the fumes)

back here
you get to see

everything

grandfathers

it is summer
I am in class
my book is thin
with brown pages
like tissue
the words are not in English
the professor is not American
he speaks of the classics:
Hussein, Mahfouz, Idris . . .
they are the greats
one day you will read them all
he speaks of philosophy
whose words I cannot understand
I daydream

I am nine years old
with my grandfather
inside his favorite book shop
which smells old
he speaks of the classics:
Fitzgerald, Hemingway, Faulkner . . .
they are the greats
one day you will read them all
he pulls thin-spined books
from the shelves
they are filled
with brown pages
like tissue
he piles them into my waiting arms

I am still in class
the teacher speaks of greatness
his words are not in English
but I understand them
on the corner of the thin white book
with pages like tissue
are pictures
of men in blue robes
surrounded by black letters
my grandfather could not read
I devour them in his honor
spit them back in English
in his memory

di dove sei?[1]

most people
have a simple answer
a one word
that conjures home

most people
don't get nervous
dread this question in any language
need help with the answer

I don't have
a Here
or There
that tells my truth

and I've noticed
people don't want a long story
when they're just trying
to make conversation

one warm afternoon
on the Ponte Vecchio
a solution lands on the tip
of my very flexible tongue:

la luna[2]

I practice my new answer
with everyone I meet

1. where are you from?
2. the moon

(except Arabs
because they're okay with long stories)

for days
people (men in particular) laugh
at my clever response tinged in mystery
they ask all the right questions:

did you come by rocket?
are there more at home like you?
can I come visit your homeland?
from what I've seen it is beautiful!

one evening a few days later
Marco gives me a ride home
on his motorcycle
grabs my wrist after I get off

di dove sei? he asks
I get my answer over with quickly

la luna

it is almost dark
his face is handsome in the shadows
I see him looking deep into my eyes
I am about to melt

allora, sei lunatica[3]
he bursts out laughing

3. so you are a lunatic

I feel my face burn
stammer *grazie* for the ride

buona notte, bella
he says letting go of my wrist
e ciao lunatica
he shouts just before driving off

home

as a young child
when Home
was where you lived
and *where-are-you-from?*
was more about your parents
I thought
I belonged
to the Whites
because that
was where
my house was

I pretended
those children
with chisels
in their powdery hands
and spit in their wet pink mouths
didn't mean to hurt me
as they questioned
my name
my face
my place of birth
my father's absence

later
when I stared
in the mirror
examined my skin
peeled it back
peeked through
at tissue and veins

and blood
saw who
I really was
I opted
for the Arabs
erased all
whiteness
erased my house
let those warm
dark arms
hold me
love me
make me theirs
build me
a new house

it worked
for a while

until I found
that Home
is inside
not out
that the view changes
depending
where I sit
which window
I look out of

mixed blood
is like an old trailer
that's always frowned at
because no matter where

it's parked
it's always
out of place

on the other hand

you can drag it anywhere
if your hitch is strong enough
just be careful
if there's a hurricane
or tornado
yours
will be the first to go

browner shades of White

under *Race/Ethnic Origin*
I check *White*
I am not
a minority
on their checklists
and they erase me
with the red end
of a Number Two pencil

I go to school
quite poor
because I am *White*
there is no
square to check
that I have no
camels in my backyard
that my father does
not have four wives
inside the tents
of his harem
or his palace
or the island
he bought
with his oil
money

my father is a farmer
my mother is a teacher
I am *White*
because there is no
square for *Exotic*

my husband
does not have a machine gun
though sometimes his eyes
fire anger
because while he too is *White*
his borders have long since been smudged
by the red end
of a Number Two pencil

my friend who is *Black*
calls me a *Woman-of-Color*
my mother who is *White*
says I am *Caucasian*
my friend who is *Hispanic/Mexican-American*
understands my dilemma
my country that is a democratic melting pot
does not

Air Force visitors

for Vasudha

boiling desert summer
singed our toes
burned our souls
pumped blood hot and heavy
into every curve of our developing teenage bodies

while our parents worked
we paid a neighborhood hotel
for membership to its pool
so we could cool our bodies
in the beautiful blue water
watched over by a lifeguard
whose face I couldn't remember even then

stranded between girl and woman
content in a discontented teenage way
we dove and jumped and splashed
then stretched out on chairs
to tan our bodies that peeked out of suits
too tiny to accommodate eastern figures
eastern standards
would have shamed our eastern fathers

one weekend the hotel filled with Air Force officers
old enough to be our fathers
they were playful, splashed and jumped
threw us in the water
as the lifeguard watched from afar

that summer I kissed a man twice my age
near the ice machine
he was muscular and short and dark
and he liked me enough
that he never did more
than kiss me near the ice machine

there are three kinds of women
he told us
there are beautiful women
there are ugly women
and then there are you two

since neither of us saw ourselves
as women
beautiful
ugly
or otherwise
we took it as a compliment

twenty years later
the details are lost
all that remains:
a faint memory of a kiss
near the ice machine

on going to the movies with a Jewish friend

1990

1
___

a new summer

out of the bookstore
into a movie theater
with *the enemy* at my side

we were close
as we sat in darkness
our elbows touching
mine and *the enemy's*

we traded glasses
to see which frames
best suited our Semitic features
they were not dissimilar
our glasses
or our features

they're dusty
he whispered
as I put his frames
around my eyes
in the safe darkness

I winced
at the blurs on the screen
he turned away
embarrassed

2

far away from my tennis shoes
lies the Palestinian shore
where my bare feet
beat a memory into the earth

distant from this smoky pool hall
is the mulberry tree
under which I wrote poetry
for that stolen shore

far from the clamor of Springsteen
there weeps a sad melody
whose audience
is the wind and the mulberry tree

unknown to my companion
is the poppy-dotted hillside
that taught my soul to breathe

3

if I were heated wax

that covered your body
from the peak of your head
to the tips of your fingers
to the ends of your toes

then sealed

would you scream my truth?

what if I melted again
poured myself into your cupped hands
like raindrops
would you drink me?

if my teardrops
filled a riverbed
became an ocean
would you swim with me?

if the kohl from my eyes
traced a line around you
trapping you
would you accept my heartbeat?

if I offered you my tongue
to wrap around your own

would you speak my words?

silhouette of two women drinking coffee

for Houri

they sit in jeans and drink their coffee black
the tall one pours her broken romance through a sieve
the words, while cardamom in flavor, are in English

many afternoons they meet at this café
to talk of home (to which there's no return)
and the sting of longing that permeates each day

the mood is soft, the laughter not so strong

their heads are leaning inward; the shorter woman sighs
her hands are silent, her head turned away
as she speaks with orange blossom–scented words

the angel I believed was always here has flown away
leaving me to cope alone with love that's in a different tongue
I understand too well to misinterpret

letter to my brother

one night just after 11:00
when you were 19 years, 5 months, and 8 days old
my tiny mother squeezed me out in a Beirut hospital
while our father slept peacefully beside your mother

do you remember that night?
did you feel your universe shift just a little?
did your dream capsize?

how at 57 can you tell me everything?
how at 37 will I ever know you?

I will start by looking
under your tidily clipped fingernails
inspect the peelings
caress your skull
count each hair that matches mine
I might check your teeth
for hidden stories
unfold your hands
hold the palms against my own
the way children do

could such a detailed inspection reveal the past?
could it fill me in on 57 years of living?

pull back your lip
let me swab your DNA
prove that it matches mine
that we are the same
split shortly after my birth
you in your right place

I too far away
always longing for mine

how at 57 will you ever know me?
how at 37 can I tell you everything?

a lifetime spent longing
for my real self
for a view I can breathe
for a world I understand
the truth came too late
my footprints are stained in English
my clumsy shoes large and American
can't change them now
can't cut off toes to make them fit
stuck outside
peeking in windows:
an invention
a fiction
someone who can visit but never stay
always on the outskirts

first birth decided your life
last accidental birth decided mine
we are not so different
both shaped by our father's
inheritance
inaction
inability to do the right thing
and more so by birth order
his
yours
mine

là
où Dieu nous plante
il faut savoir fleurir

or

wherever God plants us
we gotta find a way to bloom

exile

we fold ourselves into airplanes
and leave behind
our souls

we teach our tongues to do acrobatics
our grandmothers
would have thought obscene

our feet take giant, awkward steps
stamping new footprints
into steamy asphalt

our breath is sour
with plenitude
and distance

a call to Irbid

the Jewish family from whom I rent
sleeps behind these walls but I shout
8,000 miles in Arabic anyway
and Amal shouts back several good mornings
though it is midnight where I live
                    we race
each other to spill news of the past months:
work, school, American politics
my publications, impending visits

ten minutes finishes quickly
                    my room
regains its midnight silence
                    her news
told me an aunt in Tabariya
is dead, sending her father
across borders of routine cavity
searches, to his home he's allowed to visit
once a year if lucky
                    two months have passed
without any news of his return
as if he were in America, and I
were across the river visiting relatives

freedom fighter

in memory of Rashid Hussein[1]

silence chased him around the house
half way around the earth
two times
two times
four times
so many times that he now says "many"
when asked how often he has moved

loneliness is his provider
in a war with treachery
thieves
liars
cowards
countless other unsavory types
who have designed a frame for his house

happiness instills in him fear
for himself and anyone who could love it
taste it
breathe it
caress it
make a living trying to produce it
when there are more important issues at hand

pictures provide him a profession of sorts
in that he paints them

1. Palestinian poet who was born in 1936 and died in exile in New York City
in 1977.

says them
dances them
cooks them
bleeds them out of his soul with a pen
he brought with him on his first trip

words come to love him
in the darkest hours of the night
at dawn
noon
sunset
anytime they can find him home
drinking and waiting for a dance partner

identity card

for Raik

sharp blue sky
walked above the lady
who rumbled home
from market
with bags of rice
eggplant
cauliflower
a falafel sandwich
for her son
who waited
at the bus stop
to help
his mother
carry her
groceries
home

sharp blue sky
wrapped around the boy
who flew away
to a different land
ate
their knowledge
until he was
sick
puked
it up all
over them
and lost

his identity card
for extended
absence

sky got tired
went gray
got cold
stole his hair
not his memories
pushed
him inside
a yellow box
on wet streets
dawn
morning
noon
dusk
night
so the lady
can bring
eggplants
cauliflower
no falafel sandwich
the yellow box
is so far away

one day in upstate New York

the air was gray with traffic grease that clung
to the clothes and faces of passersby

the foreigner was waiting at the stop
red letters spelled *To University*
each morning, early, he waited for the bus

the ride was long and normally he'd study
but not that day; his heart thumping loudly
he chose instead to look through the window
in hopes of seeing flowers that would paint
over the grayness and calm his heart
that was now shouting at the other passengers

they reached his stop; he rose, walked to the front
smiled, and said good-bye to the driver
he took ten steps, then stopped and tried to breathe
his heart refused to work
                he fell: a heap
upon a sidewalk in America

for some minutes more he lay, alone
before he died
               all that's left: some books
a jar of pennies, and grief his wife, son, and friends
will wear, always, a cloak of gray that can't be dyed

handfuls of wind

this summer I caught handfuls of wind
at 65 miles per hour
in Kentucky
and imagined
that the air in my hand
was laced with orange blossom
that the billboards were not in English
and that you were next to me

your memories are piles of silk:
colorful and unraveled
in a heap
like your promises
I keep in a mother-of-pearl box
with the turquoise earrings
you gave me at birth
to ward off evil

one summer I caught handfuls of wind
at 120 kilometers per hour
in Amman
and imagined
that you were not taking me
to the airport so late in a night
that tasted of whiskey
and that you would be next to me

your memories are photographs:
black and white
on my desk
like my stories

that I carry with me everyday
with the turquoise ring
you gave me at birth
to ward off evil

good morning

in memory of Joe Bolton

you woke up a sigh of America in me

a week before I met you, my feet
were pattering down hillsides
clambering up mulberry trees
carrying me to the well for water—
the tasty kind for tea and company
a scarf covered my hair from curious eyes
when the sun fell on it, it burned
I kept silent for that is the way

admonitions followed me to the airport

I heard them all the way across the sea
to my mother's land of democracy
baseball, and home invasions; I cried
for the mulberry trees of my father's land
longed to nestle in soft earth when I found myself
in this place where life can eat you whole
where your neighbor shoots
your dog for waking him up at night

then you introduced yourself

said hi with no ulterior motive
behind your grin that filled my days
of summer as it brought forth poetry
I ate your words like vitamins
wrote about all those things

—aches, distance, exile—
that are everyday to me
you told me to keep going

I woke up today a world away

remembered you, your face, your
words, your anguish that carried you
away, left me in my room with
72 pages of *days of summer gone*
I want to make sure you know
I still take the one-a-day pill
sit in a corner of my room
to paint for you my distant world

cheating

for B

I love you
was scribbled
on the corner of your tongue

when you held me
the script
dripped
down my shoulder
seeped into my skin
made me smell of lies

even as you loved me
you chased countless women
all wearing the scent
of your beloved America

everything was a victim of your sabotage:
your studies
your business
love
me
your
self-
hatred contorted your vision
poured your drinks from dawn till dusk
pushed you into gay bars so you could tempt men
dragged you out holding my hand
so you could again proclaim your undying love

when you held me close
closer than any human had ever held me before
I could feel the jagged lies
poking through your designer jackets
I smelled the expensive stench
of your self-destructive nights

but I was too young
or too hopeful
to let go
so I held on tight

a moonlit visit

also for B

up before dawn
I peek out at the full yellow moon
read a page or two for inspiration
glance at the author's picture . . .

your eyes stare back
sitting across from me in my quiet house
your long fingers resting on my table
your soft brown eyes gaze at me

more than twenty years has passed
since your lanky east
stretched out on the green lawn
of our Midwestern college

though we were close in age
I was younger, innocent, optimistic
never a heroin user or abused child
I was your clean self
in penance
you often made me cry
on your way to becoming my best friend
confidant in all matters
my other half
but never my boyfriend
in the American sense of the word

you led a double life then
West and East

drinking, sex, and parties
with them
politics, stories, nighttime walks
with me

fingers entwined
we walked in the rain
up the steps of a cathedral
swapping tales of the moon and lovers
made them ours
you fiddled
with the heavy silver ring you always wore
God's message scribbled across it
(for years it amazed me
that for all your drinking
you never lost that ring
God never forsook you)

it took three years of walks and talks
of sleeping side by side
as brother and sister
for you to tell me you loved me
eastern style
like in folktales
even as you loved woman after woman
western style
like in movies
had sex with that tall blonde girl
behind the bushes by the dorms
locked yourself up for days
with the giggly Jewish girl
who went through several Pakistani boyfriends
but when I arrived early for a visit

you wouldn't open the door for me
until you had put on a shirt
would not let me walk alone
to a friend's house in early evening

eastern love in the West
even the Midwest
is tiresome, more so when it reeks of liquor
cruelty and suicide threats
how many times
did I empty your glass
take you home
tuck you in to sleep off your self-loathing?
how many times
did I listen
as you plotted
your own death?
still too innocent
to understand that some things
cannot be undone
or fixed

it took years to break free
untangle myself from
your knots and snarls
shake off those long fingers
that held me just barely above the surface

the moon this morning
your eyes in that novelist's face
seeing you sitting at my table
I missed you terribly

went searching for you in cyberspace
but there were only wispy traces

are you dead?
or back in Pakistan
or in Las Vegas or Texas
with an American wife
or sleeping with men
or sticking needles in your arm
as you did once
long ago

or have you
always been here
with me
my other self

my lost Majnoon[1]

---

1. *majnoon* means crazy; *Qais and Laila* (also called *Majnoon Laila*) is a classic seventh-century love story in which a man loses his mind over unrequited love.

love thing

I adore my poetry teacher
I announced to my mother
upon my return to America
and my subsequent enrollment
in a poetry class

I'm sure it's not love
it's your language thing
she replied, perhaps horrified
that I had made a hero
out of a Kentucky drunk

I always knew it
she said months later
after I declared my admiration
for Malcolm X and Spike Lee
you have a Black thing

your mom is wrong
the skinny kid from southern Illinois
told me a year later
you don't have a Black thing
you have a hick thing

it's a layover
from your Kentucky-poetry-teacher-thing
my mother said
about the skinny kid
from southern Illinois

I hope this is a temporary thing
she gasped
when I told her
I was quitting school
to paint houses

my Armenian friend laughed
when I told her
about the painter
with the smiling eyes
who had inspired my career change

you do have a hick thing;
it's part of your blue-collar-idealistic thing
maybe that's why I am so happy with this man
who has dancing eyes and no country
and made his living driving a taxi in New York City

in the pockets of my dresses

for Raik

today I began to take
my words about you
string them together
on silken thread
place each colorful beaded chain
in the pockets
of my jeans and dresses
so that if one day
your smile should seem less friendly
your eyes dance less as they watch me
your calloused hands not feel so gentle
I shall still have
beautiful strings of words
born when love was first born
spelling stories
around my neck
warm surprises
with a pinch of love
in the pockets of all my dresses

your country

I think sometimes
that if I were your country
you wouldn't be tired
in the evenings
you wouldn't leave
crumbs on the floor
and you would always
make sure I was happy

if I were your country

I sometimes wonder
if you were allowed to have
your country in some way
more substantial than
adding a gold charm
to my necklace
if you would treat it
the same way you treat me

I also wonder
if I were scented
in orange blossom
not French perfume
if you would compose songs for me
in honor of my springtime

would you fold my cotton dresses
the way you might fold your flag
if you were allowed to show it?

would you hold my face between your hands
as you would with the earth of your country?

if I were the wind
I would sneak between your fingers
behind your ears
across your eyes
tickling you
until you turned to embrace me

February

though it has just started to be February
the air tastes of summer
my lips are salty
and I spend the sunny days
peering down at memories
in other places
every summer past
piled beneath me

at the bottom:
my first fifteen years
June through August
in the big white house
that stared down
the Atlantic Ocean

in the middle:
macaroni and cheese and red wine
with my best friend
artichokes with my mother
peaches, watermelon, sour cheese, grapes
in my newly reclaimed country

then further up:
beer, cigarettes, tequila
dancing with friends

closer to the top now:
furious talks with my father
translated into crazy scribbles
with a southern poet

all different years
now one giant summer
remembered in February
at the beach—the Pacific this time—

I watch the sun paint my baby's dark face red
wear him out
collapse him into a heap
delighted with exhaustion
the kind that comes only to children
only in summertime
except in L.A.
where it comes on February 7th

motherhood

I teach my inner-city days
to act suburban
forget the sky above
lock away the heart within

focus on
price adjustments from the Gap
asparagus at $1.99 a pound
polyunsaturated fat

to hush the scream
I paint my face with the latest hues
and dress my feet
in a funky style

I take daily walks
of at least twenty minutes
while pushing a stroller
for maximum cardiovascular benefit

I numb my passions
with Ajax
Parents magazine
and homemade soup

but I cannot change
the station
to which my soul
is programmed

sitting in traffic, or zooming along
to the next destination

I let Marcel Khalife
Fairuz, even Omar Diab

plead with me to go back
down a road less traveled
with a greater hope
and a better view

home, again

curvy roads
face west
watch the sun set
face east
watch the laundry dry
south is the house on the hill
north is the eldest
brother's mansion

forty years old
educated
married
children
you're done

carry your longing
in two suitcases
nestled between
cds and zaatar
coffee and tea
enormous platters
made in china

what she's trying to tell you
is that there is no need
to pay attention
to yourself
you have done your part

final video snapshots on the way to the airport

for Raad and Rabiah

laundry folded
bags packed
watermelon eaten
its stickiness washed off
your hands and faces

though it's five hours
before our flight
and should be
a one-hour drive
to the airport
it's time to go

every cousin is here
dressed-up
to say good-bye

it's different
for each of you

with relief and dread
you try to smile
turn away
from your aunties' tears

while *you,* with no words
for your sadness
run and jump and scream
and chew through your shirt

good-byes call
out the house
onto the porch
down the stairwell
onto the road
into a taxi without seatbelts

sulky fig trees
stuck in red earth
wave farewell
windows on stone houses
beckon your quick return
gold leaf tips
on black iron gates
railing-less balconies
stone steps
are all silent witnesses
to your departure

quick stop
to another cousin
for a plastic bowl
of fresh plums
that bleed on your thick lips
wafts of
bread smells
a last reminder
of belly-filling meals

windows down
catch cat screeches
dog barks
and two mosques

that compete
in their calls

turn back to see
laundry squeezed together
flapping farewell
satellite dishes
black water cisterns
clustered on rooftops like women
wondering who you will marry
steady conversations
observing your leaving
into a breath-stealing sunset

forward now
over speed bumps
potholes
no shocks
bounce you
thump you
bang out your sadness

put your face
against the window
so the tiny curtain
tickles your ear
and watch
electric wires hanging slack
like jump ropes
heavy with waiting
black plastic bags
snagged on dried
prickly grasses

clusters of lights
winking

pass check-points
onto a highway
smooth and fast
like home
you both doze
until the airport turnoff
where our taxi
is flagged to the side
where you look away/into
the eyes of soldiers
who check your passports
(the fifth time)
dust your cousin
for explosives residue
strip him and his taxi
check for bombs
you both watch fingers
resting on the triggers
of machine guns

wide awake now
back into the taxi
to drive for one minute
dropped at the airport's door
only to be picked out again
stand to the side
while your father
nervous now
because we are late
shows passports

tickets
explains destinations

watch us answer questions
zigzag into this line
that line
unzip this bag
unpack that suitcase
explain these containers
latex hands grab
everything
I took hours
to stuff in
leave it for me
to repack quickly

run faster now
as you hear
your last name
mispronounced
across the whole airport

four airport officials
shout as you run
why are you late?
you hear the spit
in their voices
you see the glares
from many passengers
as you are
the last ones to board

settle into seats
both of you exhausted
in your new traveling shirts
we are all ready to go home

except your father
who looks very sad

home (one last time)

is the letter *qaf* pronounced like a *g*
too sweet tea and gazes that linger
my hand that catches wind, dust, and memories
                at 120 kilometers per hour

Palestine is only home when I am away
Jordan is home when I am there
I can claim neither
                except in stories

eid

the day starts with my brother's drunken slur
pouring across thousands of miles and an ocean
to wish us *eid mubarak*
while the TV shouts behind him
drowns his empty promises
(second cousins to those of my father)

> home sits above the bellybutton
> below the heart
> waits for a familiar lilt
> a certain accent
> to pry it out of its deep slumber
> float it to the surface
> a benign lump at the throat

we laugh about his 15-year-old son
who drives around Amman
with the bass in their SUV thumping
across neighborhoods
unfamiliar with gangsta rap

> all it takes
> is the tiniest unexpected phrase
> a gentle touch
> the smell of my grandfather's shaving cream
> the wet of sand between my fingers
> the sweet taste of flat Pepsi
> to pry it open
> a giant internal organ
> with no room to stretch itself

in the evening
over kifta
rice
and Scrabble
our Syrian friend
his Apple Pie wife
their red-white-and-blue children
constructed American happiness
tinged in Islam
with a hint of Arabic

    unleash the *ghurba*[1]
    I feel it rising, large and fierce,
    filling me with an evil mood
    a deep sadness for my tiny son
    who cannot bear school
    for my exiled husband
    who cannot find happiness
    in this land
    of too many opportunities

we leave their scrubbed-clean-of-longing house
all four of us grumpy
haunted by unfulfilled memories
that force home
under cushions
with crumbs
quarters
and other lost treasures

1. homesickness/alienation

yesterday

life overwhelmed me
as it sometimes does

I took the children
to their tennis lesson
stripped down to almost nothing and ran
with music of other people's exile
pounding in my ears
thumping with my heart's beat
keeping my knees from giving out

I ran against traffic
in clothes tighter and smaller
than I've ever worn
in my twenty years of running

felt free and alive and strong

by the third mile
I had forgotten the clothes
stopped thinking about the looks
I'd get
I'd give
to someone dressed like me
just ran away
from every single thing
that was pressing down on me
pulling the muscles in my back
into the tightest knots

when I had no more breath
I threw my leg against a fence

stretched from here to Palestine
stepped down and threw the other leg against the fence
stretched from Jordan back to here
plopped down into the grass in splits
that reached around the world

all while my children slammed yellow tennis balls
across green turf

after a reading by Khaled Mattawa[1]

1
---

your place in the world is solid

my place in the world moves
without a schedule
is based on mishaps
unwanted affairs
political discord

my place drifts
between Here and There
West and East
sometimes gets lodged
In-Between

my place is a Somewhere
that cannot be found
on any map
was detached
as I was born
in a place that belonged
to neither of my parents

can't be an immigrant
if you haven't left somewhere
can't be a native
if you're from somewhere else

1. a Libyan poet living in the US

which is why I'm fluent in the language of exiled souls

my place in the world
got misplaced like luggage
sometimes on clear days
or smoky nights
or during peace marches
or poetry readings
I remember the fine leather
the soft but durable hide
the confidence in the brass handle

my place peeks out during certain questions
who is your father?
are you related to the queen?
where is Palestine?
questions that can't be answered
by someone with no place
no wreckage to trace
all gone-before-me generations

2

my place re-relocated
with the arrival in airplanes
of 19 foreign nationals

my tent packed itself up
in the spitting face
of evangelical Christianity
vanished like Merlin
ebbed away
each time George W. Bush spoke

lost its permanent residence
misplaced its green card
folded itself up origami-like
catapulted into the cosmos

I know it is somewhere
drinking coffee
drinking whiskey
watching satellite TV
writing a poem

last night
when you told your story
in that sweet voice
that wrapped around
English, Arabic, French, and Italian
like a member of the Ringling Brothers
my place popped out
between your words
under the shadows of your accent
next to your kind laughter
coated in the forgotten protocol of eastern greetings

it doesn't matter that you are a stranger
you're not really
you're a reflection
a visiting relative
to my Somewhere In-Between
telling your story
my story
in lines that wooed some
confused others
with words that embraced me like a grandmother

like a lover
and for 58 minutes
brought me back
to my own
true
place

colors

under desert sunsets
my mother painted my soul orange

(I am fluent in orange)

there was a time when I bathed
myself only in black

(I tried to cover up her paints)

I shouted dark purple, brown,
and blue when they came to mind

(it stained our house)

deep bruises seeped into the tree wells
and out to the street

(that ugliness got old)

I flew across oceans and gardens
and mountains

(collecting the sun's paintbrushes)

now I carry my words like colors
in my head and paint stories

(on all the blank walls I can find)

my grandma and your grandma
were sittin' by the fire . . .

letter to an Israeli soldier

July 23, 2006

Dear Mr. Israeli Soldier,

Normally in letters I start out by wishing the person to whom I am writing good health and spirits. I would, if I knew you, send good wishes to your family and for your work. I am not going to do that as I do not have even the edges of good wishes for you, though if I were a diplomat or a politician I would say that I do.

I am writing to you today because I want to tell you about a village, one you may or may not have passed through in a heavily armed and armored jeep (was that you I saw when I was walking back from the well with my family?) You have not bombed this village. Recently. Yet. Nonetheless, you need to see it. Close-up.

The village (don't for a minute think that I'd be so fool as to tell you its name!) is nestled among soft hills and some houses are lucky enough to catch the breezes through their windows. To get there takes some patience and I probably saw you along the way, perhaps at the airport (*you get your own welcoming service,* exclaimed my husband's nephew) or at the bridge (*you set off the alarm one more time, you don't come into the country*) or at the entrance to our *gated community;* you are everywhere, considering this country is not yours. In spite of all that, the air here has a thickness to it, a warmth. Maybe because it is holy air. The village we are going to, over bumpy pot-holed roads, has houses made mostly of white stone; some are simple one-room buildings, while others are villas with several stories. Like many villages in the area, there are myriad fig and olive and almond trees that surround the houses. Some have archway entrances that are covered with purple bougainvillea. The earth is thick and rich and delicious looking.

You know, there are far too many homes and buildings and other things to describe and I'm sure you're in a hurry, so why don't I just tell you about one house. Yes, I think that's a good idea. I will tell you about one house. That one, up there. Let's pass the corner grocery store and go up the hill and turn into that little driveway. This house is about seventy-three years old (yes, older than the state of Israel) and sits on a good sized plot of land atop a hill so that at night its occupants can see the lights of the town (and of two of your outposts) and can feel the cool summer air, now not so fresh and rather stained with blood and arrogance. It has a few simple rooms and has recently been remodeled so that its kitchen and bathroom are modern with new and shiny tiles.

Come to think of it, I'm not an expert on architecture. Instead of telling you about the house itself, let me tell you about the people in it. That is a much better idea.

Depending on the day, you will find relatives who span four generations. They include a social worker, a clothes store owner, an illiterate mother/widow/grandmother/great-grandmother, a librarian, a hairdresser, many mothers, a taxi driver, an electrician, another social worker, an author, a few students, a salesman. And the children! There are a lot of children. Perhaps I should just tell you about them. Adults are adults, after all, each with his or her own stories/problems (one of the social workers is from a refugee camp (1948) and has diabetes; the taxi driver (who was just beaten by soldiers. You?) has a wife who is about to give birth; the electrician (beaten, arrested and released) can't find work; the librarian is trying to do home repairs before he returns to his home abroad).

There is a thirteen-year-old girl who sometimes wears a red baseball cap and likes the Blues. Her eyes are very dark, her skin is smooth, and she is soft-spoken and kind. She has a little sister with dark curly hair, gold hoop earrings, and a bright, infectious smile. They have an older brother who has just discovered his body in that way of teenage boys, and who walks around with his thick muscled arms stretching the sleeves of his T-shirts. They have another older brother who has spent the last year in college in Egypt studying accounting. These four have cousins who have lived in America and who have moved back. They have other cousins who are visiting for the summer. There is one boy with flirtatious thoughts of one day becoming president of the United States.

Please stop laughing now. It is an impossible hope, isn't it? I know. Impossible. I won't tell him that though, won't erase the dream of this brilliant Palestinian boy who is growing up in the United States having the gall to dream of being president. He doesn't know yet that there is a different set of rules for Arabs.

Sorry, I was digressing, wasn't I? You're still laughing? You know what? I don't want to talk to you about these innocent children. I don't feel that you are being respectful enough.

Next door there is a woman who plants flowers so that she can help her children to focus on the beauty of life, so that they can be surrounded by good. If you pass her house, and go through the empty field and up the road you will find the house of a woman who has just quit smoking and who is feeling stressed and sad in a way that is common to people who have just quit smoking. Her mother had been visiting for the summer but is now gone and her husband has just been turned back at the airport. (You must be familiar with this practice, Mr. Israeli Soldier, this new attempt to divide families, not allowing them to stay more than a few months if they have citizenship from elsewhere, not allowing them to come back more than once a year, though this is their home. If only you enforced this rule on the Jewish foreigners—there would be no settlements!)

The woman's daughter has just completed her first year in university, and has sonorous laughter that fills a room, fills an empty heart. She is tall and her great-grandmother tells her that she is too fat. She spends hours a day sending furious e-mails to friends about the state of things, about the destruction you are creating in Lebanon, about the humanitarian disaster you are causing in Gaza.

Unlike her Lebanese and Gazan brothers and sisters, she has the luxury of an ample food supply, of roads being passable (checkpoints are nothing compared to no roads at all), of explosions being merely distant and sporadic.

Around their house is a garden, with fruit trees and herbs and flowers. Tending to these living things gives her mother peace. Their house is spotless, shiny clean, and filled with knick-knacks and pictures. From the kitchen window, where you would stand to do the dishes, is a view of the northern edge of one of your settlements, one that sits on land that belongs to their family. When the woman who lives there looks out the kitchen window, she does not stare at the identical slanted red roofs protected by American taxpayer money, instead she looks at the bright sky above, on which no one has yet staked a claim.

Let's wander around the village and meet some other neighbors. Maybe go into the city and meet the principal of the boys' school and his wife who works at a fertility clinic. No? You don't have time? I understand. Well at least you have these few snaps. Here, let's tape them together and make a panorama. (I realize that I could do this digitally, but if there were a power outage, we would lose everything.) There. What do you think? There's the village, then the house, then the people. It's a good collage. Oh look, all the people we've met are sitting on the veranda outside. They're drinking sweet mint tea and singing. Have you heard that song? It's a silly song about a short skirt and it has everyone clapping and laughing. Perfect. That picture goes right at the center of our collage.

Do you have it? Yes, hold it up like that. Good. This is my gift to you, and I would like you to hold it in front of you as you sit in your tank or your ship or your F-16, or wherever it is that you launch your missiles from, aiming at strategic targets, whether they be Hamas or Hizballah, or an entire family celebrating their children's successful school year on the beach. I want you to look at the faces (especially the four-year-old with the incredible smile) and hear the joyous laughter (the tall university student) as you aim. I want you to look into her eyes as you get ready to launch your American-made missile (and don't worry if you run out of them; I hear Mr. Bush is sending you more, special delivery), as you feel the rush all soldiers talk about as it barrels away from you at hundreds and hundreds of miles per hour.

Take one last look at the faces. Each time one of your missiles sails through the air in an excruciating display of force, those are the faces at the other end, the faces that in an instant will be splattered on white stone walls and ceilings, on flowers and rich earth, on sand and car upholstery, and on mothers and fathers. Limbs flying across dining rooms, dining rooms crumbling into the ground. These are the people filling the cars that are trying to escape, the ones with the white flags that you bomb because you are sure they are hiding terrorists. The civilians you told should leave. I know you know what I'm talking about.

I have taken too much of your time, Mr. Israeli Soldier, so I will leave you with this final thought, one that we all learn as children:

In the eyes of God, we are all equal.

refugee

in memory of Saad Abu-Saud

the lungs of the wrinkled gray-eyed man
bellow with love
for a dusty quarter
of land
that lies a stone's throw
from the rock
where he sits every day
and watches
his neighbor
his fields

the path leading up here is beaten
with his dreams
mixed in the lonely dust
every day
you will find him there
with tears
racing down his cheeks
as he bleeds
a river
to take home

August 16, 1990

she's having an Arab-thing
the neighbor lady once said of me
as though my father were temporary

my mother had an Arab-thing
I wanted to say
and I'm the leftovers

now the neighbor lady and my mother
speak together
about the problem with the Arab-thing
which has now become an American-thing

you're sympathetic
the neighbor lady tells my mother
because you have an Arab-thing
I'm sympathetic because I'm a pacifist

she's sympathetic because it's a horrible situation
I shouted in silence to the neighbor lady
who would never have an Arab-thing
because it could only be temporary

a day at the park a few days Before

March, 2003

glossed-up pink mouths
talk loud and fast
about husbands
discount buying clubs
cloth diapers
diaper rash
good schools
test scores
due dates

these statistics
flatten the day
into circles
of chatter
where minivans
sleep patterns
poop patterns
eating preferences
refused vaccines
are the order of business
where any emptiness of the soul
is translated into
purchasing on-line
Gap quality
at discount prices
forgotten pedicures
longed-for massages

a solitary father appears
will there be a new set of topics?

the self-conscious
mother-of-three
smoothes her hair
her legs
her tummy
but remains
thick
and maternal

the two tightly-jeaned
hiply-dressed
mothers watch him
as they race each other
with anecdotes
about their
son
daughter
baby
perfect productions
and sources of endless
conversation

one paints a picture
of her completely
dilated cervix
the other struggles
to pull out
a breast
bursting with milk

the father keeps his eyes fixed
on the children climbing
on the yellow-and-blue jungle gym

as he chatters about his son's fear
of dogs

there is no mention
of the war
that's coming
no impending loss
fear of the world's destiny
shock at our arrogance
Indian-movie-misery

those thoughts
are stashed
somewhere else
smothered
by routine

or lack of interest

penmanship

the Iraq war, day 4

it's all mapped out
planned like a trip
from start to finish
(a trip to Hell)

anticipation loosens
bowels, tempers, missiles
shit flies
officers throw grenades
tantrums
and it's all part of the plan
the scheme
the reinvention
of the Middle East
(middle of what?
east of whom?)

money holds the pens
has all the relocation
done by people
who have never heard
of Mont Blanc
and would think it ridiculous
to waste that kind of money
on a pen, no matter
how powerful the ink

ashes and dust and fire
spew overhead

dribble down
knotting themselves
into people's lungs
like hatred

beautiful fields
are still beautiful
only now they're littered
with shrapnel and death,
the kind that makes people
see crooked
breathe rage
swear revenge

rage

the Iraq war, day 6

I am angry

at everyone
for not doing enough
to stop this

I am numb

with fear and sadness
for everyone involved

mostly I am impotent

which is why this safe school
for little children
is a blessing

where people say
how are you?
and mostly mean it

the Brazilian teacher
leans outside, smiles
you guys okay?

my rage quiets
throughout the sweet morning
filled with giggles

digging and singing
crackers and popsicles
stories and cuddles

is all but forgotten until
we are headed to the car
and I am ambushed

not by a right-wing
pro-war
evangelical Christian parent

who questions my nationality
worries about
our connections

but by a well-traveled
liberal mother who stops me
puts her hand on my arm

as you would
to someone who is grieving
and quivers
I'm outraged

then tells me
about the gourmet dinners
she arranges
with fellow liberals
to discuss her disgust

I need like-minded people
what an awful,
sickening, grotesque display . . .

though I see her anger is genuine
perhaps a reflection of my own
her designer words

make me want to spit

bundles of toddlers
climb the wooden equipment
in front of us

she points and shakes righteously
these children she says
and you can see she is struggling
with her own fury

these children will
not be able to travel

her words have found the keyhole
to my locked-up anger
which is purple in color

red in volume

children just like these
won't be able to live!
shouts my voice in puce

decorum broken
I carry my three-year-old
to safety

away from my unfolded fury

away from abstract
visions of war
and destruction

away from liberal mothers
and their intellectual
outrage financed by

working husbands
American dollars
and discussed over

white china plates
of marinated kebob

demonstrators

one thousand
one hundred
one
it doesn't matter the number
they came
and walked
for peace

we joined our fellow citizens
to voice dissent
and have a good walk

my children carried signs
(peace, please)
and looked earnest
my mother held their small hands
my co-worker smiled for the crowd

waify girls
in black velvet
carried a coffin
with the words
500,000 Iraqi children
painted graffiti style

there were peace signs in English and Arabic and Spanish
(no Hebrew)
people carrying oleander branches
(not olive)
marching along tidily
(no South African bouncing)

the Palestinians in front of us had a drum
to give a rhythm
a beat
for feet and shouts
and occasional laughter
(nervous levity)

a group of unshaven young businessmen
(purposely scruffy for the occasion)
tempted the police
by crossing the yellow line
then smiled at the crowd
encouraged enthusiasm for their daring

veterans and grandmothers and hippies
and preppies and women with their hair covered
and women with their bellies uncovered
carried pictures
and signs
and babies
and hope

all trying to save a nation
or two
or a thousand

it doesn't matter the number

intentions

eyes lock
mine on his
or his on mine
I'm not sure who started it

American
so proud
that he added two more years
to the two years he already served overseas
leaving
his business
wife
two sons
classmates/teammates
of my older child
which is how I know him

but I don't really know him
barely speak to him
because of his aloofness
or shyness
or affiliations

it doesn't matter
not everyone can be best friends

he's back now from Qatar
or Jordan
or Iraq
or whichever Arab country he was sent to
where I have friends or family

but this time I see him changed
more permanent somehow
like he figured out how to tattoo America
inside his clear blue eyes that stare deep
not with lust or friendship
deeper than that, more under the skin

he's looking for recognition
wants us to thank him
for all that he's doing for us
suggests a friend

I don't see that
when our eyes meet
lock
crash
I feel fingers
probing for my heart
or blood
or soul

like he wants to say something
about where he was
what he saw
something important
and he knows that I will listen
that I can debrief him

for a minute
I catch myself
watching him
not my youngest son
who runs in front of him

just as he kicks a soccer ball
sending him head over heels

he gently picks up
my sobbing child
holds him tightly
so sorry for what he's done
when I take my son
out of his arms
I cannot look in the soldier's face
not until later
when the tears are dried

he is watching, smiling
not with lust or friendship
but with satisfaction
like someone who just climbed a mountain
because it was there

refugee (of love)

since a few years after
my country went to war
I have been secured
behind barbed wire
returned to my birth status
of non-citizen
eight years now
stuck in a refugee camp
not allowed across any borders
turned away
from any rightful home
living in limbo
alone and forgotten

I've escaped twice
been given rudimentary refuge
by neighboring nations
a silky tent
a sleeping bag
bottled water
basic sustenance and a little hope
but when it was clear I wanted to stay
I was returned to this desert
my home away from home
the best one can do in times of war

tonight I think I can make it out
if it is God's will
I have a plan
to sneak through that fence
disguise myself

as one of them
work my way back
to the main road
then it's home free
in a matter of speaking

they say third time is a charm

my anticipation is tidal
filling me with fear
and excitement
blinding and terrifying
more exhilarating
than anything I've known
since long before
the war began

it was the guard's idea
the giggly one
who asks for cheeseburgers
I think his name is Ali
was he trying to help me escape
or is he just too free
with his words?

as the hour approaches
doubt creeps in
how can I trust this Ali?
I've known him
little more than an hour
he has no business
offering me a way out
or even hope

how do I know
he's not trying to trick me?

the answer comes clear:
trust in your heart
tell no one

short video clip: Baghdad tattoo

November, 2006

the room is cramped and dark
except for the table on which a man sits
with three naked bulbs shining

over a rectangle of shaved hair
credit card in size
etched onto a pale slab of his thigh

the middle-aged artist
comes out of the shadows
to begin his work

his face has three days of dark stubble
and he looks like he smells of smoking
he leans over his subject and begins

no naked woman takes shape
no mythical beast, gang affiliation
cartoon character or lover's name

the ink from the artist's steady hand
forms thick, tidy letters:
name, address, telephone number

the man whose thigh is exposed
looks at the camera and clears his throat
so my family can identify me—

thighs are less likely to be destroyed

taking a moment to thank our sponsors

CNN is advertising dark meat
stacked in a heap
a prime-time display of flesh
never to be sold at Safeway
a humiliated stack
of military training
gone digital
a slab of trailer park
meets Mossad
no leftovers
just prime cuts
whose bloodline can be traced back
to before time
when there was proof of God
before the age of pixels
and Guantanamo
before Texas
before Pilgrims

this is what's underneath
the candy-coated hatred
whose crinkly wrapping has ripped apart
its thick Disney paper torn
its Hollywood tissue in shreds on the floor
its evangelical dye in a puddle
surrounding a man on a leash
held by a cross-eyed woman

outrage pours from the lips
of pundits as the scenes unfold, unwrap, drip
into our consciousness
as we read

this is an anomaly
such things happen in war
American soldiers are apple pie
fighting for the freedom of the Iraqis
fighting terror
terror
terror
terror
terror
terror
that tattoo stitched between the legs
of each and every American
never mind that there is no umbilical cord
attaching this country
this war
this stack of men, hooded, leashed, posed
to the nineteen men
shaved and clean
who staked out planes
until they thought they had God's permission
to perform the ultimate test
of the Emergency Broadcast System

never mind the last few years
decorated in Texan democracy
bordered in box cutters that have ripped out
the hem of dialogue
understanding
history
bringing us to this lip
of destruction
brought to you not on al-Jazeera
but on CNN

could be Beirut

July, 2006

1. day three

air here is thick and hot

the monsoon moisture
soaked into the asphalt
sizzles up like a sauna

Friday is when
my children and I
walk two miles
up and back
to rent
a movie

but my toe is broken
and it's killer hot
so we drive instead
listen to the radio
hear the news
about bombs
exploding
in Lebanon

we listen
safe in our car
not trying to escape
to anywhere
pull up
to the video store

as they talk
about the staggering heat
in the Midwest
and the Middle East
(finally they have something in common)

we go inside
look for a family movie
without violence
end up with *Tom and Jerry*
a cartoon I met in Jordan
my children in Palestine

our cashier
is older and more competent
than most of the other employees

she looks at me over her reading glasses
as she types my information into the computer
we can't keep this place cool today
she says pointing at the entrance behind her
with that door swinging open constantly
today is particularly bad

I agree with her
though talking about hot weather
in Arizona
in the summer
gets old

I guess it could be worse, I say
thinking about the broadcast we just heard
we could be in St. Louis where it's humid too

she's scanning our video
or Haifa, she says without looking up
as though this is her reference point
as though it is a given that anyone's sympathy
should be placed there

or Beirut, I say
because she clearly needs some perspective

she looks up at me and squints her eyes
as though
she has just seen
me more clearly

due back Monday

the three of us exit
into the stifling heat
cross the steamy asphalt

she is still watching

my sons keep looking back at her through the window
Mama, is she supporting Israel's bombing?

I don't answer
we pile back
into our car
safe and air-conditioned

return home
to watch
our movie

2. day nine

don't answer the phone
or reply to e-mails
keep the curtains closed

Mama, stop being sad

read the news
watch the footage
spend the day red-eyed

Mama, can't you stop?

scribble your words
the ones
that feel like vomit

Mama, let's go to the pool

for just one hour or two
let it go
it's okay to forget

3. day ten

power outage
106 and climbing

my family
has gone

to the bookstore

the house temp
is rising

but we are not in Beirut

forty minutes later
power is restored

and everyone
comes home

safe

**a warning to all Arabs traveling back to the United States:
TSA officials are now employing Israeli security tactics
at the Newark airport**
or
**now would be a good time to go dumpster diving
at Newark Liberty International Airport**

three weeks ago
my brother-in-law and his wife
returned to the States
from a trip home

like every Arab
they packed as much
of home as they could fit

one suitcase
stuffed with spices
dried cheeses
coffees
teas
homemade
sweets

when they were asked
if they had anything to declare
like everyone
they lied
a truthful lie:

they carried no seeds to plant
no wheat to harvest
no fresh items

no living plants
roots and mud still attached
nothing for sale
nothing alive

just one suitcase
intended to stave off
homesickness
for another year

Newark airport officials
confiscated every single bag
of tastiness
every tin
every container
every single one
of those wonderful things
that make coming back tolerable
fined them three hundred dollars
for lying

about . . .

three cleaned-out
dried-in-the-sun
soda bottles
stuffed with dried *mlukkhiyya* leaves
a spinach-like vegetable
that calms the exiled stomach and soul
(and smells like marijuana when it's burned)

two clean plastic bags
filled with zaatar

deadliest of all mixtures
made from dried thyme
sesame seeds and sumaq;
dipped with bread in olive oil
it could create explosive happiness

dried tea leaves
best coffee
in Ramallah
lethal items
might keep you up at night
plotting to maintain your employment

we're here
in no man's land
no land for this man
this Palestinian
deserves no place
hounded there
spit at here
there is no longer
home
no zaatar to dive into

close your eyes
imagine that life
turned out
as you had planned

homeless
with two homes
home away from home
visitor

always visiting
no settling
here
settlements
there

impossible
afternoons
thank God
alcohol
is *haram*
or we'd be like
the Indians
homeless
and hopeless

this way
it's just
limbo
all
just
temporary

that prick
of light
of hope
farther
away
than
ever

strange men in my house

1. November, 2001

a preppy man
representing the Nielsen family[1]
rang our bell, showed me ID

I unlocked our security door
and let him in

we would like yours to be a Nielsen family
he said in an easy voice like soap
I ate up his squeaky clean story in one bite

two months ago
all Arabs came under suspicion
but all Arabs did not become suspicious

not yet

I ignored his excitement about our satellite dish
his interest in our ability to hear bin Laden's statements
before they have been translated

I provided him with all sorts of personal information
social security number, husband's college degree, current place of
    employment
so he could check us out

---

1. The Nielsen company monitors household television viewing to determine
audience size and program preferences.

he promised boxes of cookies for the kids, a chance to skew
     America's viewing
even offered to install another phone line for free
so the Nielsen family could always be connected

for months
a box would be installed in our living room
tracking viewing
viewers
conversations
intimacies

finally
a *Sopranos* kind of vision of an old van filled
with scruffy men wearing headphones
unfolded in my mind

my husband gasped at my gullibility
my non-conspiracy-theory-believing mother questioned Mr.
     Nielsen's veracity
my children asked for the cookies

I called and canceled
forfeited our chance to rate America's shows
to put al-Jazeera's news programming right up there with
     NYPD Blue

viewing is not proof of political affiliation

not yet

2. February, 2003

Arabs may be under suspicion
but now we are interesting too
it is time for our voice to be a part of America's ethnic fiction

out of the clear blue
that matches the paintings in our house
and a couple of pieces of furniture
my manuscript is picked
chosen
opted
edited
copy-edited
proofed
cleaned up
blurbed
and streaked in Blue

I am interviewed
by the *New York Times*

they send a photographer, a fashionably scruffy, normal man
who arrives in the rain and rings the bell
I open our security door
and let him in

he makes me laugh as I turn this way that way
knowing my hair is flattening and I should not smile too much

the blues are fantastic, he says of my dining room table, painting,
    and teapot

click, click

we drink tea together, almost chums

do you mind if I use the bathroom? he asks
of course I don't
and while he's gone I think how familiar and compatible and very
        funny he is

it is not until later after he's gone that a nagging voice in my head
whispers:
if it seems too good to be true . . .

like an addict who's lost her stash
I dissect the bathroom, pull back cabinets, open drawers, check
        under the toilet
for a bug

the kind you see planted on TV in the *Sopranos* or *NYPD Blue*

insane, says a voice in my head
too good to be true, says another voice

one and a half years ago, all Arabs came under suspicion
today all Arabs are suspicious

I find
no bug

it is hidden too well

homeland security

1
-----

the government has no sense of irony
my friend tells me
when I call to report on the activity next door

are you sure they got the right house?

early this morning
just after I returned from my run
cop cars filled the empty spaces
squashed the morning silence

armed men and women clad in bullet-proof vests
stomped up the next-door neighbors' concrete driveway
bordered by orange and red annuals
thumped onto the covered porch shaded with wisteria
pounded on the blue door until they roused the fifteen-year-old boy
who was asleep in his boxers

they dragged him into the street in handcuffs
shoved him in the back of a waiting patrol car
let him sit there

while the father and stepmother
who had been on their way to exercise and meditate
were escorted back by three squad cars

(one is never enough)

must be drugs
my friend said

2

during the next seven hours
the boy was returned to the house
allowed to get dressed sit with his stepmother
while his father was questioned

uniforms from three different agencies
dumped the house
went through papers
clothes, trash, furniture
pulled back books
furniture, dishes, food
looked under couches
animal cages
figurines of the virgin Mary
Buddha
Shiva
Ganesh

shook up peaceful vibes
dropped their crumbs on the floor
commented on the fine architecture
tasteful arrangement
of furniture

interrogated each person
separately
together
waving a warrant
that included a clause
stating only a lawyer
could petition

for the right
to see the reason
for the early morning raid
a petition
that could
and would be
denied

so the focus was on the boy or his parents?
my friend asked
still unbelieving

are you sure they got the right house?

3
___

the next day
my neighbor came over and said she had no idea why they had
    come at all
that they had asked questions about their travels
their e-mail accounts
and the money they send
to Buddhist organizations

she's lying
my friend said

they must know and it probably has to do with the boy
who's either dealing drugs or porn

and I still say the government has no sense of irony
to dump the house next door to Arabs

don't they know who you are?

an open letter to president-elect Barack Obama regarding the situation in Gaza

December 29, 2008

Dear President-Elect Obama,

Belatedly, I congratulate you on winning the election.

Belatedly, I offer my condolences for the death of your beloved grandmother.

Hopefully not belatedly, I implore you to consider your role in Palestine.

Though I try to avoid watching the news, last night I forced myself to look at coverage of Gaza. I started with CNN and Reuters, and though at that point over two hundred Palestinians had been killed, the footage I saw was of the funeral for the one Israeli who died. I watched several men carry a coffin. I saw attractive women crying. It was both public and private and one felt their grief. The message was clear: one Israeli death is one too many whereas more than two hundred Palestinian deaths are in a different category.

So I decided to watch al-Jazeera. Do you ever watch it? Shireen Abu Aqleh, who has been reporting from the Occupied Territories for the last eight or so years, is looking very, very tired. I forced myself to watch the scenes of destruction, the ambulances, the men and women slumped over the bodies of their family members. I forced myself to listen to the screams, the wailing.

I forced myself to watch these images because I feel that as long as my country is supporting the country that has caused this, I am guilty.

I got to thinking about your campaign and my reasons for supporting you:

You were by far the smartest and wisest candidate.
Your plans were clear and intelligent.
Your ego did not get in the way.
There was another more personal reason.

I also supported you because you are familiar.

Like you, my mother is White and my father was brown and foreign.
Like you, I had a funny name.
Like you, I did not grow up with my father, but his absence shaped the person I became. Like you, I had connections abroad, an entire other world that seemed as though it should in some way belong to me. Or I to it.
Like you, I was, at times, an Other.
Like you, I became very good at gauging situations and people.
This is why I trust you.
Why I knew you were the only candidate who would truly treat other world leaders as equals, thereby earning their respect.
Why I sang your praises over Senator Clinton to anyone who would listen.
Why I wrote letters, wore T-shirts, bought my kids T-shirts, and bought a second bumper sticker for my car after the first one was stolen. (My younger son, who was eight at the time, wrote you a letter and you wrote him back. He has that letter pinned to his door, and he was your spokesperson in the third and fourth grade.)

You see, President-Elect Obama, the familiarity that I see in you is one of fairness and justice: you can see both sides of a situation because you are both sides, and it's why you ultimately choose what is right and not what is popular. You also have a tremendous sense of history, so I know you are aware that what we see today is not everything.

Which brings me back to Palestine.

Gaza is filled with people whose family homes are being lived in by Jewish settlers from all over the world. Many of those people, if they are permitted entry back into the country that was once theirs, have to wait an hour or more for the privilege to walk by those homes on their way to working in a factory to make underwear or T-shirts for Western women. They smell the freshly mowed lawns, hear the splashing of children in bright blue pools on land that was once theirs. Most of them try to tune out the past, focus on the few constants they are allowed in this present life: family and faith.

It is never just today. Just as you are not simply a Black man in his forties who got a new job, this is not simply an explosive situation between good guys and bad guys.

Gaza is also filled with very creative people: all sorts of artists, musicians, actors, dancers, who hone their skills and dream. There are teachers and doctors and lawyers and nurses and engineers. And there are lots and lots of students who dream and hope, in spite of the fact that their options are fewer than most of us can imagine.

Gaza is filled, literally, with children who can describe the villages that were taken from their families two or more generations ago. They can tell you the number of olive trees that surrounded the house, or describe the scent of citrus blossoms that filled the air, or the old man who lived two houses down who always sang whenever he walked, and how his voice was terribly unmelodic, but what an enormous void there was when he died. They can tell you these things because their parents and grandparents are determined that they not forget; that they, in turn, will not be forgotten.

It is never just today. Just as you are not simply moving into the White House in a month, refugee camps are not ancestral homes; populating a country that was already populated can involve unacceptable tactics.

Just as we took the time to get to know you, to understand your history, and to believe in you, I ask you to stop looking at today, at what is wrong with today, and to look at how it got that way.

Just as we took the time to get past your funny name, your foreign father, your all-over-the-place upbringing, I beg you to do the same for Palestine.

Until the wrongs of slavery were admitted, there was anger and extremism.

Until the wrongs of occupation are admitted, there will be anger and extremism.

And fathers and mothers like you and like me will continue to live through what is unimaginable.

I will close with something Mohandas Ghandi said, something I know that you believe:

"A confession of errors is like a broom which sweeps away the dirt and leaves the surface brighter and clearer."

very sincerely yours,
Laila Halaby

the end